Magic Science Tricks

by DINAH MOCHÉ

Author of
*What's Up There? Questions and
Answers About Stars and Space*

Illustrated by Lisl Weil

SCHOLASTIC INC.
New York Toronto London Auckland Sydney

Contents

ISBN 0-590-41704-5

Text copyright © 1977 by Dinah L. Moche. Illustrations copyright © by Scholastic Books, Inc. All rights reserved. Published by Scholastic Inc.

12 11 10 9 8 7 6 5 4 3 2 1   7 8 9/8 0 1 2/9

Printed in the U.S.A.

11

Light

Electricity and Magnetism

Chemistry

Models to Make

The Magic Science Show

This is a different kind of magic book. In it you'll find 29 science experiments that are so amazing, you won't believe what you see or hear the first time you try them. What's more, these are real science experiments, that prove strange but true facts about the world around you.

After you've done the experiments yourself, try putting on a show for your family and friends. In this kind of magic show you can give away the secret — that's part of the fun. When you tell your audience how the tricks work, they'll think you're a SCIENCE WIZARD! (You don't have to tell them it's all in the book.)

The directions for each experiment are easy to follow, and you will have most of the equipment you need around your home. But if you don't, you can buy what you need at a 5¢ and 10¢, toy, hobby, or hardware store.

After your first performance of Magic Science Tricks, you will probably think of some ideas of your own to add to a show.

A warning!

Safety is very important in every science laboratory. All the experiments in this book can be performed safely IF you follow the directions. Read all the directions before you start each experiment, and be careful as you work.

When you see one of the symbols below at the beginning of an experiment, turn back to this page and read the special warning.

 Get permission to use the stove or hot plate. If you don't know how to turn on the stove or hot plate, ask an adult to help you.

 Be especially careful with matches. Get permission to light them or ask an adult to help you.

 When you are mixing chemicals be very careful not to splash any of the liquids on yourself or on the table where you're working.

 Get permission to use the iron. If you don't know how to use it, ask an adult to help you.

Wherever there are safety warnings be sure to pay attention to them.

Now turn the page and have fun.

Gravity

A Good Party Trick

Tell your friends that you can drop a penny and a paper napkin and make them hit the floor at the same time. They may not believe it, but you can do it.

You need: *a penny; a paper napkin.*

Here's what you do:
Crush the napkin into the tightest little ball you can make. Then hold the penny in one hand and the napkin in the other. Raise both your hands to the same height over your head. Count down, and let go. The penny and the napkin will hit the floor at the same time.

Why it works:

Gravity pulls all falling objects down to Earth. It pulls all objects the same way — no matter how big or heavy they are, or what they are made of.

An *un*crushed napkin will fall slower than a penny. Air pushing up against the surface of the napkin will slow it down. If there were no air at all, an uncrushed napkin would fall as fast as a penny.

There is no air on the moon. Astronaut David R. Scott tried this experiment on the moon. He dropped a hammer and a feather together. They hit the ground at the same time.

The Race Against Gravity

Here's something everyone in your audience will volunteer for: catching the dollar bill.

You need: *a dollar bill*.

Here's what you do:
Ask for a volunteer from the audience. Have the volunteer rest his arm on the table, with his open hand over the edge, as in the picture. You hold the dollar bill between his parted fingers and thumb. Make sure that half the bill is held above his hand. Tell the volunteer to grab the bill as it falls. But DO NOT announce when you will let go. No one has been able to catch the dollar bill yet.

Why it works:
Gravity *accelerates* falling objects. That means that gravity causes falling objects to move faster and faster as they fall. The dollar bill is pulled through the volunteer's fingers in about ⅛ of a second. No one can grab the dollar bill that fast. The eyes, brain, and fingers must all get the message that the bill is falling before the person can grab it. By that time the bill is gone.

Over the Top

Believe it or not, you can swing a pail of water upside down over your head without a drop falling out. (This is a good experiment to perform in a bathing suit in an outdoor show.)

You need: *a small plastic beach pail; water.*

Here's what you do:

Fill the pail about ¼ full of water. Swing the pail back and forth in front of you a few times to give it speed. Keep your arm straight. When you get the pail moving with some speed, quickly swing it in a circle high in the air. Remember, keep your arm straight and swing the pail very fast. The water will stay in the pail, even when the pail is going over the top upside down.

Why it works:

At the top of the circle the water in the pail is moving straight ahead very fast. It tends to keep moving straight ahead very fast. This is called *inertia*. But gravity is tugging on the water trying to pull it down. The combination of inertia and gravity keeps the water in the pail.

The Moon and man-made satellites stay in their orbits around Earth because of a combination of inertia and gravity.

Air and Water

The Upside-down Glass

This time air will help you hold a glass of water upside down. (Practice this one over your sink until you're good at it.)

You need: *a glass; water; half a sheet of construction paper.*

Here's what you do:
Fill the glass all the way to the top with water. Hold the glass in one hand. Put the construction paper on top of the glass with your other hand. Hold the paper tightly in place and turn the glass upside down. Take your hand off the paper. The paper won't fall off. The water won't spill out.

Why it works:

The air around us is pushing against everything. It pushes hard (14.7 pounds per square inch at sea level) in every direction. When you turn the glass upside down, the water inside pushes down on the paper. But the air outside pushes up even harder. Air pressure keeps the water in the glass.

Air vs. Muscle

Here's another trick with air pressure. Tell your audience that you are strong enough to lift a heavy book with only your breath.

You need: *a heavy book; a large balloon; a short piece of plastic tubing; a rubber band.*

Here's what you do:
Insert the plastic tubing (*make sure the ends are smooth*) into the neck of the flat balloon. Wrap the rubber band around the neck of the balloon. Now air can get into the balloon only through the tubing.

Put the flat balloon on the table. Put the book on top of the balloon. Blow air through the tube into the balloon. The book will rise as air fills the balloon.

Why it works:

When you blow air into the balloon, the air spreads out. It pushes very hard against every part of the balloon wall. Compressed air inside the balloon pushes with more force than the weight of the book. The compressed air lifts the book, just as compressed air in your bicycle tires supports your weight.

A Hole in the Bottle

Surprise your audience by keeping water inside a bottle that has a hole *below* the water level.

You need: *an empty plastic bottle with a screw-on cap; water; a small plastic dishpan; scissors.*

Here's what you do:

With the scissors, carefully poke a small hole in the bottle, near the bottom. Cover the hole with your finger and fill the bottle right to the top with water. Don't leave an air space at the top. Screw the cap on as tightly as you can while you keep your finger over the hole. Hold the bottle on the edge of

the dishpan. Don't squeeze the bottle. Take your finger away from the hole. The water won't pour out.

Why it works:

When you cap the bottle, air can't press down on the water to help push it out. Also, the air pressing against the outside of the hole prevents the water from pouring out. Water spills out of the hole when the cap is off the bottle because air pressing down on the water helps to push it out.

Hot Air Balloon

Let hot air blow up a balloon while you save your breath to explain this experiment. (See 🖙 page 5.)

You need: *a balloon; a Pyrex chemistry flask; a pot; water; a hot plate or stove.*

Here's what you do:

Make sure the flask is dry and clean. Stretch the neck of the balloon over the mouth of the flask. Put enough water in the pot to cover the bottom. Stand the flask up in the pot of water. Turn on the hot plate or stove. As the bottle heats up, the balloon slowly blows up. Let the bottle cool off before you take it out of the pot.

Why it works:

Heat causes air to spread out, or *expand*. When you heat the air in the bottle it expands out into the balloon and blows it up.

Heat does the same thing to the air in your bicycle tires in the summer. It causes them to expand.

Shipwreck

Create a disaster at sea.

You need: *2 toy boats; a plastic spray bottle; string; a dishpan filled with water.*

Here's what you do:
Tie a piece of string to each boat, as in the picture. Arrange the boats so that they are side by side in the dishpan. Let the strings hang loosely over the sides of the dishpan. This will keep the boats in place on the water.

Shoot a stream of water, from the plastic spray bottle, on the water between the boats. Your audience may expect the moving water to push the boats apart. They will be surprised when the boats come together in a quick collision.

Why it works:
Still water pushes harder than moving water. When you cause the water between the boats to

plastic spray bottle

move, you lower the pressure between the boats. Then the higher water pressure outside the boats pushes them together.

Because of this difference in pressure, large ships passing each other must be steered very carefully to prevent a collision.

Climbing Water

You know that water runs downhill. Show your audience you can make it climb uphill.

You need: *a paper towel; 2 glasses; water; food coloring; a large book.*

Here's what you do:

Fill one glass with water. Add some food coloring to the water. Put the glass of colored water on the table. Put the large book next to it. Set the empty glass on top of the book. Now roll the paper towel tightly, lengthwise. Put one end of the towel in the glass of water. Let the other end hang over into the empty glass. The colored water will slowly climb uphill into the empty glass.

Why it works:

Water is made of many tiny particles called *molecules*. These tiny molecules hold onto one another and move up into the narrow, empty spaces in the towel. This is called *capillary action*.

You make use of capillary action every day: drying yourself with a bath towel; drying dishes; watering dry plants in pots or the garden.

Sound

Teeth That Hear

By now your audience is about ready to believe anything you say. Tell them you can hear through your teeth. You can.

You need: *a metal fork; a metal spoon.*

Here's what you do:
Hit the fork with the spoon to make a sound. As soon as you can't hear the sound with your ears any more, put the handle of the fork between your front teeth and bite down on it firmly. You'll hear a sound again.

Why it works:

When you strike the fork you make it vibrate so quickly that it makes a sound. Air carries this sound to your ears and you hear it. Solids like teeth and bones conduct sound better than air. When you put the vibrating fork against your solid teeth, you can hear the soft sound.

Hearing aids, worn by some people who are hard of hearing, use the bones behind the ears to conduct sound.

Musical Strings

Add a little musical entertainment to your magic science show with an instrument you made yourself.

You need: *4 feet of nylon fishing line; a wooden board about 10 by 10 inches; 8 medium-size screw eyes; a block of wood about 1 inch square (1" by 1") and 8 inches long.*

Here's what you do:

Put 4 screw eyes part way into the board on one side. Put the other 4 screw eyes into the board on the other side — directly across from the first four. Cut 4 strings from the fishing line to stretch across the board between the pairs of screw eyes. Tie the ends of the strings around the threaded stems of the screw eyes — not through the holes. Tighten the strings by turning the screw eyes. Put the small block of wood under the strings at one end.

Pluck the strings to make a sound. Change the pitch of the sound by making the strings tighter or looser. Or you can move the screw eyes and make the strings longer or shorter.

Why it works:

When you pluck the strings you make them vibrate. The vibration causes sound. The pitch of the sound depends on how long the strings are, and how tightly they are stretched. Now you can design and play stringed instruments that make sounds you like. Violins, guitars, banjos, and cellos are all stringed instruments.

Water Horn

Add a water horn to your musical instruments.

You need: *a small funnel; an empty can; water.*

Here's what you do:
Fill the can almost to the top with water. Hold the wide end of the funnel part way under the water. Blow across the top of the funnel stem. You can rest your lower lip against the stem as you blow. You'll make a different kind of musical sound than you did in the last experiment.

Why it works:
Blowing air across the funnel stem causes the air in the stem to vibrate and produce sound. The pitch of the sound depends on how long the column of air is. If you change the water level inside the funnel stem, by pushing the funnel up or down, you change the length of the air column. This changes the pitch of the sound. Wind instruments, like flutes and horns, make music this way.

Light

Mysterious Message

With a mirror, you'll read a secret message.

You need: *a sheet of carbon paper; a mirror; 2 pieces of writing paper.*

Here's what you do:
Lay the carbon paper on a table with the carbon-side up. Put both pieces of writing paper on top of the carbon paper. Ask someone from the audience to write a message on the top piece of paper. Then tell that person to remove the top paper and throw it away.

Now you turn the second piece of paper over. You'll find the message written backwards on the back of the second paper. Hold this paper in front of the mirror. You'll be able to read the message easily in the mirror.

Why it works:

You have no trouble reading the words on this page because light rays are going from the letters directly to your eyes. But when you hold writing in front of a mirror, light rays go from the letters to the mirror and then to your eyes. The mirror sends back, *reflects,* those light rays. Reflection makes everything look reversed.

Sign your name above the backward message. When you look at it in the mirror it will be reversed.

Money-making Mirrors

Mirrors can make you look rich. Tell your audience you can turn a quarter into a dollar — just by using mirrors.

You need: *a quarter; 2 mirrors.*

Here's what you do:
Put a quarter on the table. Hold the mirrors together on the table so that they make a V around the quarter. When the V is wide open you see a quarter in each mirror *and* the one on the table. Slowly bring the mirrors closer together. As the V gets narrower, you will see three quarters in the mirrors. If you want to "make" even more money, bring the mirrors closer together.

Why it works:
Light rays from the quarter hit the mirror. These light rays are reflected back and forth by the mirrors before they go to your eyes. Reflected light rays let you see more than one quarter in the mirrors.

Copy Cat

Copy your favorite picture — or ask someone in the audience for a picture to copy.

You need: *a piece of glass about 8 by 10 inches (picture-frame or window glass); a piece of white paper; a pencil; a lamp; a picture.*

Here's what you do:
Put the picture you want to copy on the table. Put the piece of white paper next to it. Hold the piece of glass upright between the paper and the picture. Shine the light from the lamp onto the picture. Look through the glass and you'll see an image of the picture on the white paper. Hold the glass firmly and copy the picture.

Why it works:

You see an image of the picture behind the glass because some light from the picture goes to the glass first and is then reflected to your eyes.

Bent and Broken

This bit of science magic will teach your friends not to believe everything they see.

You need: *a pencil; paper; a ruler; a glass of water.*

Here's what you do:
Draw a dark straight line across the paper, using the ruler. Hold the paper behind the glass so that the line is on a slant. When the audience looks at the line through the water, the line will look bent and broken. You can straighten the line with no trouble at all. Just remove the glass of water.

Why it works:
The audience sees the ends of the line through air only. They see the middle of the line through air and water. Light travels faster in air than it does in water. The light coming through the water speeds up when it gets into the air. It also changes direction. This is called *refraction. Refraction* makes the line appear bent and broken.

Make a Rainbow

Let sunshine help you put on a rainbow-colored light show.

You need: *a mirror; a pan of water; bright sunshine.*

Here's what you do:

Put a pan of water in a place where the sun can shine on it. Place the mirror in the pan so that it is under the water *and* leaning against the side of the pan. Position the pan so the sun is shining directly on the mirror. Move the mirror slightly until you see a row of colors on the ceiling or wall. If you do this outdoors, use a large piece of white paper to catch the colors.

Why it works:

Sunlight looks white. But it is really made up of red, orange, yellow, green, blue, indigo, and violet light — all mixed together. These are called the colors of the *spectrum*.

When the sunlight moves into the water at a slant, it slows down and its colors separate. When the sunlight is reflected back through the water, into the air, the colors are separated even farther apart and you can see them clearly. This is just what happens in a rainbow.

Electricity and Magnetism

Needle Magnet

With sewing needles you can point out the direction to the magnetic north pole of Earth.

You need: *2 sewing needles; sewing thread; a magnet; a glass bottle; a ruler; paper, 2 by 3 inches.*

Here's what you do:

Rub one end (pole) of the magnet along the first needle about 30 times. Rub from the eye to the tip of the needle each time. Rub the other needle in the same way with the same pole of the magnet.

Fold the paper in half. Push a needle into each side of the folded paper as though you were sewing (see picture). Have the tips of the needles pointing in the same direction. Make a small hole half way along the crease in the paper. Knot the thread and push it up through the hole. Tie the thread around the ruler. Let the paper hang from the ruler down into the bottle.

At first, the needles will swing back and forth. When they come to rest, they will point in the direction of Earth's magnetic poles.

Why it works:
By rubbing the needles with the magnet, you turn them into magnets. When you let the needles move freely, they are pulled toward the magnetic poles inside the Earth.

Lights On

Light up your show with a switch you make yourself.

You need: *a 1½ volt dry cell battery; 3 feet of bell wire; a flashlight bulb and socket; an aluminum foil baking pan; a block of wood about 3 by 5 inches; 2 flat-head nails; scissors; a small screwdriver; a hammer.*

Here's what you do:

Cut a strip about 3 inches long by 1 inch wide from the aluminum foil pan. *Be careful not to cut yourself on the edges of the metal.* Nail one end of the strip onto the block of wood. Do not hammer the nail all the way into the wood. Lift up the other end of the strip. Hammer the other nail into the wood *underneath this free end.* Again, don't hammer the nail all the way in. Now you have a switch.

Next prepare 3 connecting wires. Cut the bell wire into 3 pieces, each about 1 foot long. Remove the covering (insulation) from the ends of all the wires so that about ½ inch of bare wire shows. Now you are ready to connect them.

Wind one end of the first wire around one of the metal screws on the battery. Wind the other end around one of the nails on your switch. Connect the second wire, in the same way, to the battery and

the socket. Use the screwdriver to loosen and tighten the screws on the socket. Connect the third wire to the socket and the other nail on the switch. All connections must be tight.

Press the free end of the aluminum strip down on the nail. The light goes on. Lift the aluminum strip. The light goes off.

Why it works:

The bulb lights up when electricity flows through it. Electricity can only flow if it has a complete path, called a *circuit*. When the metal strip is touching the nail, the circuit is complete. When the metal strip is lifted off, the circuit is incomplete.

Switch On-Switch Off

Experiment with some other materials to see if electricity will flow through them. Your audience can take part in this.

You need: *the switch, battery, flashlight blub, and socket from the last experiment; pieces of plastic, cloth, silverware, nails.*

Here's what you do:
Remove the aluminum strip from the switch. (p. 42). Press the material you want to test firmly against both nails. If the light goes on, the material has electricity flowing through it. If the light doesn't go on, electricity is not flowing through the material.

Why it works:
Some materials let electricity flow through them easily. They are called *conductors*. Metals like copper, silver, and aluminum are good conductors. Materials like plastic, rubber, and cloth are poor conductors. Electricity cannot flow through them easily.

The Sometimes Magnet

Now it isn't — now it is!

You need: *a 1½ volt dry cell battery; 10 feet of bell wire; a nail about 3 inches long; paper clips or tacks.*

Here's what you do:

Wind a few layers of wire around the nail. Leave at least a foot of wire hanging at each end. Remove the insulation from both ends of the wire so that about ½ inch of bare wire shows. Connect one of the ends of wire to one of the screws on the battery. Connect the other end to the other screw on the battery.

Now the nail will pick up paper clips, tacks, and other small metal objects. To save the battery, be sure to disconnect the wires when you are finished with the experiment.

Why it works:

When electricity from a battery flows through a wire it makes magnetism. The nail wrapped in wire is called an electromagnet because it is a magnet when electricity is flowing through the wire. You can make your electromagnet stronger by wrapping more wire around the nail.

Chemistry

The New Penny

Make some old dirty pennies look like new. (See  page 5.)

You need: *white vinegar; salt; a small glass jar; measuring spoons; dirty pennies; water; a towel.*

Here's what you do:

Mix 3 tablespoons of vinegar and 1 tablespoon of salt in the jar. Put the dirty pennies in the jar. In a few minutes they will be clean and shiny. Rinse them in water and dry them.

Why it works:

The chemical name of vinegar is acetic acid. The chemical name of table salt is sodium chloride. When you mix vinegar and salt you make hydrochloric acid. Hydrochloric acid takes the dirt off the pennies.

Fire Fighter

You can't see it or smell it, but you will know it is there when the flame goes out. (See  page 5.)

You need: *baking soda; vinegar; a small glass jar.*

Here's what you do:

Put 2 teaspoons of baking soda in the jar. Add 2 tablespoons of vinegar. Bubbles and fizz rise in the jar. You have made carbon dioxide gas. When a lighted match is put into the jar, the flame goes right out.

Why it works:

Baking soda and vinegar are chemicals. When they are mixed together, carbon dioxide gas is formed. Carbon dioxide gas does not burn. Because it is heavier than air, it does not let air get into the jar. A match can't burn without oxygen from the air. Because carbon dioxide gas doesn't burn, or support burning, it is used in fire extinguishers to put out fires.

The Color Clues

Do a little detective work now. (See 🗒 page 5.)

You need: *5 or 6 red cabbage leaves; a cooking pot with cover; a mixing bowl; a wooden spoon; a potholder; baking soda; white vinegar; water; 3 small glass jars; a stove.*

Here's what you do:

Before you start your detecting, you'll have to do a little preparation. Put 5 or 6 red cabbage leaves and 2 cups of water in the pot. Cover the pot. Bring the mixture to a boil and let it simmer (cook on a low flame) for 15 minutes. Let it cool, then pour the purple juice into the bowl. Squeeze out extra juice from the leaves with the wooden spoon.

Now you are ready to perform. Take the three glass jars. Put 3 tablespoons of white vinegar into the first jar. Put 3 tablespoons of clear water into the second jar. Put 1 tablespoon of baking soda and 3 tablespoons of water into the third jar. Stir until the baking soda is dissolved.

All three jars look alike. They contain colorless liquids. Now comes the magic. Add 2 tablespoons of the cabbage juice to each jar and watch the color changes. The vinegar will turn the juice red. The baking soda will turn the juice green. The water won't change the color of the juice.

Why it works:

Red cabbage juice is called an *indicator*. It changes color — red when it is mixed with an acid, green when it is mixed with a base. Scientists can tell by this color change whether a substance is an acid or a base. You can test some of the liquids you drink — soda, milk, lemonade — to find out whether they are acids or bases. If the cabbage juice turns the liquid reddish it is an acid. If it turns it greenish it is a base.

RED   PURPLE   GREEN

Crystal Garden

Make a crystal garden to show your friends. (See ⚗ page 5.)

You need: *5 tablespoons of salt; 1 tablespoon of household ammonia; 6 tablespoons of water; a jar; several small pieces of charcoal (or brick); a stick; food coloring; a plastic container.*

Here's what you do:

Arrange the pieces of charcoal in the plastic container. Mix the salt, household ammonia, and water in the jar. Stir the mixture thoroughly with the stick to dissolve the salt. *Be sure not to splash any liquid into your eyes.*

Pour the mixture over the pieces of charcoal. Dot the pieces of wet charcoal with drops of food coloring. Put the container in a warm place where no one will disturb it for several days. Check each day to see how the crystals are "growing."

Why it works:

When you let this mixture stay undisturbed in a warm place the water evaporates. Salt and ammonia crystals are left behind. The food coloring gives the white crystals a beautiful color.

Invisible Ink

You can make invisible ink out of milk. (See ⌔ page 5.)

You need: *milk; a cup; a piece of white paper; an iron; a thin paintbrush.*

Here's what you do:
Pour some milk into the cup. Dip the paintbrush into the milk and start writing with it on the piece of white paper. Keep dipping the brush into the cup as you write to keep it wet with milk. When you finish writing, set the paper aside to dry. In a short time you won't see anything on the paper. Press the paper with a warm iron. The words will appear in a dark color.

Why it works:
When the milk writing dries on the paper it is white. The white writing is invisible on white paper. By heating the paper, you burn the dried milk slightly. It changes to a dark brown color that you can easily see on white paper.

Models to Make

Weather Vane

You need: *a soda straw; scissors; a piece of cardboard about 3 by 4 inches; a pin with a big head; a pencil with an eraser.*

Here's what you do:

Cut a big triangle and a small triangle out of the cardboard. These will be the vanes of the weather vane. Make a slit, about a ½ inch long, lengthwise, in the end of each straw. Slide the large triangle, tip first, into one slit. Slide the long side of the small triangle into the other slit. Now you have an arrow weather vane. The small triangle is in front, the big one is in back.

Hold the straw with your thumb and index finger and find the point at which the straw will balance, so that it doesn't tip forward or backward. Push the pin through the straw at this point. Then push the pin into the eraser on the pencil. Hold the weather vane up outdoors. You can tell where the wind is coming from by watching where the arrow points.

If the wind is coming from the north, the weather vane will point to the north. If the wind is from the east, the weather vane will point to the east.

Kaleidoscope

You need: *3 mirrors, each 2 by 3 inches; a cardboard roll from used up paper towels; several small pieces of colored or giftwrap paper; a short wide-mouthed glass about 3 inches across; 4 rubber bands; ruler; pencil; scissors.*

Here's what you do:

Stand the three mirrors on their 2-inch sides to form a triangle. Have the glass sides facing in. Put rubber bands around the mirrors, one near the top, one near the bottom, to hold them together. Open up the cardboard roll, carefully, by tearing along the lines. Cut off a piece of cardboard about 12 inches long and three inches wide. Wrap this around the mirrors and hold it in place with the other 2 rubber bands to make a short tube.

Cut the colored paper into little pieces of different shapes. Put the cardboard tube, with the mirrors, inside the glass. Drop the pieces of colored paper into the center of the glass.

Slowly turn the tube. Look into the mirrors. You will see beautiful changing designs. Tap the bottom of the glass to rearrange the pieces of paper. Reflected light makes the patterns you see in the mirrors.

mirrors
rubberbands

Cardboard roll
2 rubberbands

small pieces
of colored
paper

1 Glass

61

Electric Question & Answer Board

You need: *a piece of cardboard 10 by 12 inches; 16 feet of bell wire; 1½ volt dry cell battery; a flashlight bulb and socket; 2 paper clips; scissors; a screwdriver; white paper; a pencil; a ruler.*

Here's what you do:

With the ruler and the pencil, mark off 10 places down the right side of the cardboard. Keep the spaces between the marks equal. Make a small hole in the cardboard at each mark. Number the holes from 1 to 10.

Make 10 more holes down the left side of the cardboard, directly across from the first 10. Number these holes, starting at the top, in this order: 9, 7, 5, 1, 4, 6, 8, 2, 10, 3. This will be the back of the quiz board.

Now cut 13 pieces of wire, each 14 inches long. Uncover 1 inch of bare wire at each end of all 13 pieces. Stretch the first wire between the two holes numbered "1." Put the ends of the wire through the holes. Turn the board over to the front. Twist the bare wire sticking through each hole into a loop to keep it from sliding out. Connect all the other pairs of holes in the same way. Make sure you connect matching numbers.

You have three pieces of wire left over. Use one of

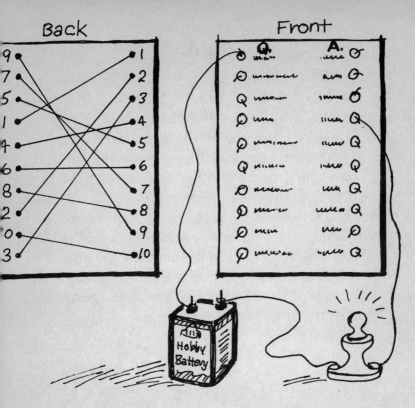

them to connect the battery to the socket, by wrapping one end of the wire around one of the screws on the battery and the other end around one of the screws on the socket. Use the screwdriver to loosen and tighten the screws on the socket. Connect the next piece of wire in the same way to the other screw on the battery, but leave one end of this wire free. Connect the last piece of wire to the other screw on the socket, and leave one end free.

Now cut a sheet of white paper to fit on the front side of the quiz board between the wire loops. Write 10 questions down the left side of the paper next to each wire loop. Write the answers to the questions down the right-hand side of the paper in this order: answers 9, 7, 5, 1, 4, 6, 8, 2, 10, 3. Do not number the answers. Clip the paper to the front of the board. Now you're ready to use the quiz board.

If you touch one of the free wires to the loop next to question 1 and the other free wire to the loop next to the answer to question 1, the bulb will light up. But if you touch one free wire to question 1 and the other free wire to any other answer, the bulb will not light up. You have to match the questions with the correct answers to make the bulb light up. If you do this you make a complete circuit and electricity flows through the wires.